Reading the Water

Laurence Hutchman

Black Moss Press

2008

Library and Archives Canada Cataloguing in Publication

Hutchman, Laurence

Reading the water / Laurence Hutchman.

Poems.

ISBN 978-0-88753-447-8

1. Water--Poetry. I. Title.

PS8565.U83R42 2008   C811'.54   C2008-904300-6

Cover Image: Marty Gervais

The 64/10 series is published by Black Moss Press at 2450 Byng Road,
Windsor, Ontario N8W 3E8. Black Moss books are distributed by
LitDistco. All orders should be directed there or write to
www.blackmosspress.com.

Black Moss Press would like to acknowledge the generous support of
the Canada Council and the Ontario Arts Council for its publishing
program.

The Canada Council | Le Conseil des Arts
for the Arts | du Canada

ONTARIO ARTS COUNCIL
CONSEIL DES ARTS DE L'ONTARIO

for Mary, Sean, and Emma

ACKNOWLEDGEMENTS

Some of these poems have been previously published in *The Fiddlehead, The Antigonish Review, Body Language: A Head-to-Toe Anthology.* "Erotic Scene at the Royal Ontario Museum" won first prize in the Writers' Federation of New Brunswick's 2006 Literary Competition.

I would like to express my gratitude to the Faculté des études supérieures et de la recherche, Université de Moncton; the Secteur Arts et lettres, Université de Moncton, Campus d'Edmundston; and artsnb, for creation grants. I would like to thank Brian Bartlett, Ronnie Brown, Charlotte Hussey, and Bill Willan for reading the manuscript and for suggesting valuable changes. I would especially like to thank my wife, Mary Hutchman, for her editorial judgement, understanding and love.

OTHER BOOKS BY LAURENCE HUTCHMAN

The Twilight Kingdom
Explorations
Blue Riders
Foreign National
Emery
Beyond Borders
Coastlines: The Poetry of Atlantic Canada (editor)
Selected Poems

TABLE OF CONTENTS

SWIMMING TOWARD THE SUN

PORTRAIT

READING THE WATER

CLIMBING THE GREAT WALL

Swimming Toward the Sun

LISTENING

This morning, over the water
a voice in the light is calling,
Star of Venus, never brighter,
a goblet in the water.
I go to the edge of the lake,
gaze over the water to the pine trees
shrouded in their fuzzy coats,
blurred against the final light of the stars.

The light, like blood, bevels on the water
over the folds of its dark body.
Here the birds call
out to one another in their unctuous cries.
Their ululating gullets, yodelling the air,
bring movement to the pines
in the nightclub of the forest.

I am discontent.
I leave this old self,
a snake skin, on the rock.
I call out to the ghosts of the past.
I call out to the wound on the water
but the lake, a balm
draws my voice down into its darkness.

Forget your adolescence.
Give voice to your pain.
Listen, now, to the birds trilling
—come closer, closer
little bird, breathe on me,

bring delight in the rustling of your wings.
On the sand bank
by the water
that shell, mother of pearl,
fading crescent moon,
a quiet ear listening.
Shed your old skin.
Listen to the water.
Listen to the light.
Here, on the shore,
listen to the bristling music of birds,
the voices of morning.

SWIMMING TOWARD THE SUN

I could not stay in the cabin.
Others slept while I stepped
out under the night sky.
How cold and damp the air.
Before me, the lake.
I step down to the rock.
I think of those who died this year.
The lake dark, heavy, cloudy.
I cry.
There is mist on the lake
curling like grief.

As I sit on the beach,
the deep sounds of the frogs,
bass fiddles, draw sounds
out of sadness; I listen to them

in the large pit of the lake
singing in tenor and bass,
syncopated in time,
and then the loons
blowing their mysterious horns
to other loons who answer them,
and the Phoebes who raise their little melodies
while large invisible fish splash like timpani.
All the sounds rise and fall in this pastoral,
orchestrating the darkness.

I swim away from the dock;
the sky is turning in the red
sandbars of the clouds and the water slowly
changes as the sun begins to break
the horizon. I swim toward it
as it sends golden rays across
the waves—and there, two loons
glide through serenity;

the sun is a great sword
swelling its sharp light
the loons gliding toward the fiery path
like the men in Nebuchadnezzar's furnace.
They disappear into the light,
glow darkly, in their colours of the lake
as I swim through.

LOON

This morning I see you
out on the water,
your long neck quilted with stars,
treading darkness, like a swan.
Why did we stamp you
on the dull gold of our dollar
and christen you "loony,"
a name kids called each other
on the school bus. Loon.
I think of you along with the moon,
la lune, lunacy of lovers.
How far are we
from your gliding
through darkness.
Yet, when you call out
a sound not human, not made by cello
or bassoon, just a sound which suddenly
shapes the hills, granite, pine,
something in us goes out to search for
home.

FLIGHT OF THE LUNA MOTH

As we wander along the path, people are singing in the darkness, when suddenly in the branches we see a lunar moth. Its movement is unexpected, you said, as it circles around our heads, flying up toward the purple halo of the glass lamp, trying to get closer to its dream, circling, moving from tree to tree like a child playing hide and seek in the darkness.

It is a green kite, flapping, gliding and sailing across the air, leaping into the darkness, guided by an inner music, like the idea of rhythmic movement in the composer's mind, flying, not aware that it could hurt itself. "They live for only two days in their maturity," you said.

On the ground before us it lies, as if it will die here among the wood chips—but just when we think that it will not get up, it jumps like a grasshopper. We move toward it, as it makes its arc over us. It returns to land on your leg, then graces your knee. I wonder will it come to me. It flies off, bumps into the wall, glides toward me and almost knowing what I want, lands on my shoulder like an amulet.

Soon, not so far from you and me, we follow its graceful dance as it scores the air, tracing its movements like a luminous thread, tying pieces of moments together, like the scenes of a storyteller. In awe we follow the dollop of its flight, until landing like a green biplane.

Six-year-old Elizabeth brings me the luna moth in her hand. I see it with its two magenta-bordered wings outspread, still breathing from its white-cocooned belly. Later, I see the outline of a wing in the wood chips, bend over and find only one single wing, soft as down.

KIWANO

The cashier at the Atlantic Superstore didn't know what you were. She thought you were a kumquat! You go by other aliases: "African Horned Cucumber," "Jelly Melon," "Hedged Gourd," "English Tomato." You are considered a decorative fruit, perhaps a maraca, gracing the edge of exotic salad bowls in executive suites at the Delta Hotel.

You are an orange blowfish, your rind spiked like that of a chestnut, rhino horns gathered at your front. Yet if I lift you carefully, you feel soft as leather, a worn baseball glove. When you were exported to Australia, you gained a reputation as a weed, an outlaw. Perusing your contours, I observe various degrees of orange.

I read you as a map of primitive oranges. I see other colours, ochre, amber, almost red like the surface canals of Mars. I close my eyes and let my fingers read your rind as one reads Braille, feeling around those horns and *monticules.* I can almost feel the wind blow over the sands, which rise like rivers under the hills of the Kalahari.

You take me into that landscape of yourself where you are protected against the marauding predators of the desert. A cactus, an aquarium, you hold water; seeds float in your green belly. You are a tough fruit, enduring, like those ancient Africans who loved you. And when they ran over the desert hills, hungry, thirsty, seeing you under the African sun, called out, "Kiwano!"

CLIMBING MOUNT BOYCE

This morning my thigh muscles are stretched
like violin bows.
Out into the morning the dusty road stretches.
Why should we climb today,
if we will not reach the summit.
We will not get beyond the tree line.
We will not arrive at that bare place
where we can put things in perspective.
The pathway is not clear
as we move up *Burned Trail* onto *Lone Pine.*

There is no need to reach the summit.
Perhaps on these lower slopes
we will find a place where the forest opens out
or there is a waterfall.

As it gets steeper and the rocks
become irregular steps, hard
on the thighs, a shaft of pain,
I think, "time to turn back."
Sweating and fatigued,
I stop for a gulp of water from the bottle.

Is that the wind we hear?
No, that is water, continually rushing.
It is in the movement upward,
increasing ache, the stretched thigh muscles,
in the changing breath, the sweat,
the unthinking state—
only the shape of the wood chips,

each etched rock, the yellow mushroom caps,
in the moss, that the path takes over,
the thinking beyond my skin.
Up the path we move.
We can hear the invisible river,
the flow from the waterfall.
It is the way I see life, moving toward an end,
a clearing, a place where I can see my life beyond
the clearing, similar to Schopenhauer's writing,
—if you live long enough and climb high enough
you can see your life like the pages of a novel,
you can see the narratives of your childhood,
the contours of the valleys—

I want to make something more
out of this walk, to find the moment breaking
over the horizon, like that recent afternoon
behind the Pitti Palace in the Boboli Gardens
where we climbed in nearly forty degree heat.

And then, the sound of the stream becomes stronger.
We can feel it flowing through the rocks,
taste the coolness in the air.
Among the black chiselled rocks, under
the grasses and the branches,
—the waterfall.

It is not what I expected,
not the waterfall the woman told us about,
just a simple stream falling through
the shiny rocks.
I get down to face the rocks and push

the bottle into that smallest stream.
I enjoy the filling.

Perhaps death
will come like this, not with the vista, but
the closeness of water,
the tingling of consciousness,
the fullness of berries and mushrooms,
each turning in the path among the arrangement of rocks,
the high trees bending, whispering
like water in the calls of birds. And you will see

the whole contour of the mountainside above,
what you could not see before,
and below the way you had come—
each moment changing place with the other.
You will see that the path led you to this place
the stream in the murmuring of the heart,
that path of those times that moved you forward
to this moment, a lighted place
in the shadow of the forest.

THE SCULPTOR

When I was seven I would sneak into my uncle's studio.
From the pail he scooped a lump of clay
which he dug from the banks of the Humber River.
I would watch as he moulded the clay into a head,
like that of a caveman.
I watched how he shaped the mouth,
the angular ridge of the nose,

the canals of the ears
and saw the chin become a chin.
I watched him form a man's head
until it looked like a real man
whose lips could almost speak.
On his shelf were other creations,
a wild elephant with raised tusk,
a bust of Don Quixote—
his wild hair, keen eyes, and wise grin.
(My Uncle Herman would have his own windmills to fight.)
He tried to give the earth a human form,
and make the river clay breathe.

FRED

When I see you lying in bed,
the bruises on your arms,
I'm aware of the resilience of your body,
the strong light in your eyes,
those fingers, with the strength of a farm boy,
that have written so many books.

You loved sports, running two miles
back to school to play baseball after dinner
sinking a basket in that championship game.
You loved to chase butterflies,
devoured the Old Testament and the New Testament,
the *Anglo-Saxon Chronicle,*
any novel you could get your hands on,
then poetry, which became your life.

You came from Centreville, made it larger,
like the eagle that glides over the St. John Valley
tracing ever farther flights.
When you wrote, how carefully you painted
the portraits of the villagers, like an old Dutch master
faithful to their character, their prejudice, their richness:
George Burroughs, Sam Stover and Ellen Waring.

Now, in your laboured breathing
I hear your voice,
gentle, engaging, curious and passionate,
how it moves like the wind to take in all things.
It is a voice of judgement, distinction, authority,
encountering and defining the darkness of the world.

I love how you translated this land,
your grandmother from Bouctouche
having instilled in you a love of French.
You understood the poetry of exile,
drew on the voices of Acadian poets
until we heard them through your words.

The philosophy in your poems,
one that does not divide the world into separate
things, but reveals life as darkness and light,
the crescent of the moon
and the corona of the sun.

Now in your last struggle
you speak courageously,
follow that path from the farmhouse
through the apple orchard down by the cedars and
the creek, out toward the big rock pile under the tree
where you can see beyond the circumference of the mountains.

WATERFALL IN THE WOODS
ABOVE SIMEONOVO

Why is it that waterfalls
are so different
here in the woods
overlooking Sofia.
I sit on the large rock,
listening as the noise of water
fills the air like the song
of rising birds.
Why is it that the river
sounds like rain rushing
through the rocks like wild horses.
Here the water falls from
two different streams,
down into different
waterfalls. It creates colours:
grey, blue, green
in a turbulence of white—
lines move into the colour of sound.
The two streams are from different
places, like thoughts
from opposite sides of the brain
that come together, singing.
As they rise into a flow,
the thought in the mind,
from a swelling into sound,
into song, into words in these
over Simeonovo . . .

THE CAVE

As we climb the tortuous path
work our way along the staggered
pattern of rocks, a natural way
for stubborn pilgrims,
Svetla reminds us,
"You must pass through the centre of the circle"
(at least this was suggested for sinners).
But where was the circle?

The uneven white steps lead into
the darkness of the cave—this is where
Ivan of Rila survived seven years
through the cold zero of winter
and the heat spells of summer.
                    I imagine his meagre existence
here in the rocky furnishings
of this cave, the darkness
and his silence next to God.

I edge slowly along the passageway;
I am uneasy in this darkness where
it is difficult to climb its rough-smooth
surfaces while my eyes slowly start to grow
accustomed to the lack of light, but no
—there's the amber moon glimmer of a candle
and suddenly I stare into the stark
face of a saint. I venture beyond the glow
of the candle as the cave narrows;
the oblique schisms of the rock's roof
close in on me and my body bends.

The cave comes to a dead end
and I slip,
grip the wet rib of a rock.
Should I go on?
The darkness grows
and the cave narrows
and I turn to go back,
but I hear voices echoing from ahead.
I decide to follow them.
I creep like a bear along these ledges,

turn, and my eyes look up to
a bubble of light, where the sky peeks
in. But how to climb this steep wall . . .
when out of the rocks the steps of a ladder
appear. To the top rung I climb,
but how to go farther.
The voices are gone.
They must have gone through.
But how? I place my palms on the edge
—the opening is too small—
of the round rock and force myself toward
the aperture, pause at the edge.
How can I squeeze through this slim fissure
and maneuver myself.
Without thinking further, I climb,
my knapsack pressed against the rock,
slowly pushed against me as I lift myself,
feel my hands on the edge
of the earth, climb out,
find myself on the path once again.

Portrait

SWIMMING NAKED BEFORE THE STORM

Alone at the farmhouse
we ran naked into the sultry afternoon;
the air was heavy as the wind blew
through the leaves. Carefully we climbed
down over the rocks, slid
cautiously into the dark water of the creek.
We called out each other's names,
       pain released into the cold current.
Water shone on your full cheeks,
as your arms encircled
mine in that dark coolness.
We saw each other as in a film
swimming smoothly as seals.
That day we tread water
in the flow of the current
aware of our movement together
under that old timbered bridge
built by your ancestors.
I watched you climb out of the water and slowly
wrap a towel around your body.
Dark clouds were gathering,
an electric charge in the air,
the leaves rustling as we ran
toward the boarded-up farmhouse.

We climbed into your grandmother's bed, waiting
for the storm—trees buffeted by the wind.
In that moment, looking into your eyes
I saw a calmness of a life I had not known.
We pressed closer together

to move beyond our troubled past
until the bedroom was not blurred
and the lamp was still,
until the thunder cracked,
the room filled with light.
Then we were slowly awake,
leaning on each other
as the room took on a mauve radiance of the sky.

THE NIGHT IS WILD

You sleep soundly.
The night is wild.
I must get up
to encounter something in this
turbulence of wind and water.
    All week we've listened to the waves
coming in to break upon the shore
—so wild I need to hold this page down.
Will the boats go to *Isla Mujeres* tomorrow?

This morning, the sea calmer,
we venture out into its waves.
They move suddenly, the great swell rising,
breaking against us as we rise on crests.
    Wild is this force which takes us;
warning flags spoke of an undertow.
The sea moves in strong waves, hidden drag,
drawing us out and in.

You venture farther out than you've ever been,
not afraid to encounter the force
of these waves as they break dangerously over us.
I warn you of a larger breaking
wave, and we brace ourselves.
It breaks around us, and then another
larger breaker—I'm thrown back, swept under.
When I surface, you're gone.
Then you emerge, laughing as you
wipe the salty water from your brow and
cheeks—ready to be swept under by the next wave.
Tonight the wind blows wildly
at the Captain's Wharf,
but it is calm in the lagoon,
on the far pier where the fishing vessels
silhouette the horizon.

You are so beautiful,
your hair swept across your forehead,
as you hold your face up to the dark
nakedness of the evening, and speak
of standing against the thrusting of the waves.
Tonight you are calm,
your face resting on your folded fingers.
In that still moment—your eyes are radiant.
The meal is delicious;
beyond the stillness of the lagoon
we hear the distant crashing of the surf.

DANCER

This morning, on the point of departure,
you suddenly appeared
in the middle of the living room
without any clothes on.
You seemed to shiver, shimmer,
wriggled your knuckles
as if you had a castanet on each finger
and were about to dance the flamenco.
I had never seen you naked
like that before,
and I shivered too.

IN A HOUSE WE NO LONGER OWN

At night rain falls through the trees,
sings like a woman in a nightclub,
falls through the leaves like a rumour of sex,
falls through the darkness into dream.
Sometimes, I awaken,
look at your face on the pillow,
your cheeks have the fullness of rose petals.
In the rain, in the dream we dance.
And who are you and who am I?
You, so young
in the way you stretch your arms
over your shoulders,
in night's slow motion
in the mist, in the rain,
in this house we no longer own.
This night we do not own anything.

LUST

Have you ever really thought of the word? Lust. A
scrabble of the libido. Let the word roll on your tongue. The
long "l" is a liquid, curving thigh; the "u" has the rich taste
of a sexual vowel, and the ending "st," a closing of the lips.

Rhyme the word "lust" with "bust." Yes it doubles. "Must" is
that inevitability of desire—turn it around and there's a hidden
"slut." Or there is "tusl," that ultimate tussle with nocturnal
fantasies. Lust. It's more than the word—a desire that is in us,
between the goalposts of the "l" and the "t."

How is it language gives rise to lust? Say the words.
Imagine them through the negligée of language: the amber
moonshine, the midnight delta, the hidden harbour, the lighthouse,
the peninsula in light—geography of desire.

STRIPTEASE

Why don't you wear something special for me tonight?
You can begin by unfolding your black fur hat
—I loved you in that hat since the first time you tried it on
in the Château Frontenac—your Garbo hat.
What are you wearing this morning?
I like how your hair falls
—you in your red gown—
you are not naked beneath it
—"naked" a strange word, as if you could be naked.
I love that word.
I love seeing you in that word,
but now it eludes me as
your luminous red gown slips over the

shape of your breasts and the lovely
raspberry shape of your nipples
—I almost forgot about the shiny black vest
—it's leather: reveals and conceals you.
I love you in black,
it brings out the wildness in you
—the delicate features of your face,
your proud arched cheekbones,
your lips pausing before words,
in silence,
held there like a moment in Bellini,
in the Villa Borghese,
and your eyebrows...
I trace them with my finger.

How still you are in black,
the soft rouge of your cheeks
—it's not the clothes, but the way they express you,
in your black vest, *soutien-gorge*, prelude
to lingerie, my coy mistress,
—you're the belly dancer of my dreams
                    —to touch your skin.

I will not stop here; for
although it's morning,
it's night on these pages.

This page is the bedroom with the candle
shining in the presence of the yellow walls.
And the music you put on, but oh,
I love that deeper music that comes from your caress
that blurs the air in its own suspended note

falling alongside my body.
I love how you light the candles,
put each one in a discrete corner of the bedroom,
to capture the interplay of shadow and light across
the curves of your body.

I would like you to wear red shoes,
those high heels—
or the black shiny boots—
(that would be the cabaret fantasy)
how you put them on, such an eloquent tease,
zipping them up
—you don't know how many ways
(and I have not always told you)
how many ways you turn me on—

—no, it's more like the rise of the sunlight breaking over
the mountains, the hills and the streams, suddenly
making me aware of the landscape of your life
when you reach
to take your black boots off—or red heels.

Whatever you are wearing tonight
you are warm in your black mink hat,
your red gown and black leather boots.
No, you've already begun to slide the boots off
and your feet, your soles,
your toes are so slender.

Lying next to you this morning
I take that lovely fur hat off,
and your face shines in the light, shows

you are not wearing your red gown anymore.
In those moments when we touch—
what can words say
only hint at the inadequacy of language.

A LETTER FROM THE WOODS

It was twilight
as I started out on the trail alone.
I want you to be here,
to breathe this air,
to stop on this old wooden bridge and stare
across the water where the reddish last light
dissolves in the darkness.
I want you here to see
            how the stalks of the bullrushes shine
and how the weeds are so wild.
It is the kind of park you would love—
to walk into the arbour of over-arching trees,
a continual surprise of alders and birches.
I want you here to see
how the path follows the river
flowing alongside its irregular bank.
Yet, if I stop, I see an overturned trunk,
the Greek myth of a woman abandoned on a rock.
Now I push through the tangled undergrowth
because something wild has caught my eye.
What are sunflowers doing on that far bank?
Not sunflowers, but great yellow faces
of flowers with little balls of seeds in their centre.
I cannot name them.

How can I bring you this wildness in these words
—I see your face, your fine cheeks,
your radiant eyes in the distance
as I move toward you on the pathway.
It is so difficult to describe the scene,
to describe the movement of this water,
to make you see it,
but your presence is here.

On this bridge between the past and present,
I pause between the places of our lives.
Looking down from it
I see the water running through the rocks toward
a future arrested in this dark uneasy twilight.
I want to say you are here,
but the silence of the forest
says only that you are not.

Reading the Water

DEVELOPING

Father worked in a darkroom at Kodak,
his work mysterious as atomic physics.
Sometimes I took a negative out of the box,
held it up to the sun
to identify my parents, my sisters, myself,
foreigners in a dark geography.

Father had his own lab at home,
a sunless spare room
where he had an enlarger, slid
the negatives under an electric eye,
clicked the x-ray machine
where the glossy paper slowly changed
—the acceleration of the cotyledons' growth,
as in a grade eight science class.

I would watch him dip
the paper into a chemical bath, move
it slowly back and forth
as if he were washing a sheet in a river,
unrolling it like a scroll
in pungent hypo solution where light
broke through—
first shapes emerging from the sea.

Paper glimmered under infrared bulbs,
barely able to see the solitary light of his eyes,
focus on his fingers

with their knowledge of the dark
as they knew the motion
developing in those cauldrons.
I saw the first elementary forms: the birth cells,
the dance of chromosomes,
the messenger RNA.
Out of these shells, curves and designs
the familiar faces of father, mother, sisters slowly appeared.

Father would hold the picture;
this ritual he performed
every night in the factory.
He did not speak about it,
but held the photograph in his fingers.
I develop these images
within the dark template of myself.

COAT OF ARMS

I see my father in his navy blazer,
the coat of arms sewn on his breast pocket.
On the crest the skeleton sits on a rock
during the siege of Londonderry
when thirteen apprentice boys
ate leather boots to stay alive
and called out, "no surrender."
Yet, for me, the skeleton
beside the castle tower
took the ghostly form of Simon Templer's "The Saint,"
a parody of Rodin's "The Thinker"
sitting outside the fortress walls.
I see my father, smiling, in his navy blazer.

THE SHELL

You look out at me from brown eyes like an orphan,
on your skin Japanese characters or Arabic script. Now
I place you in my palm, shell, sea snail. I feel you smooth as
porcelain. You are round, firm as a breast. I feel the curve of your
upper ribs where you are flecked with sand pigment from the
beaches where you have lain. When I turn you over you are the
shape of a tiger fish. Yet, rubbing my fingers, as over Braille, ribs
become keys. I hear a distant music when my father, long ago on a
beach in Port Rush, lifted you to my ear to hear the sea gurgle and
swim within your body.

And now, I am shocked, deafened and blinded by the ego of my
shell. There is no sea now. Addressing an absence: it is not you,
only myself talking. This is your marble grave. As I look within,
I see what form you might have taken, shaped by these bones and
the currents of the sea. I feel your softer brown-moist body, like
my own, inside this carapace of being.

You are not there, only the structure of your form. I feel you
in the currents, swimming among the gaudy flowers, the turbid
underwater forest with the brothers and sisters of your species. I
hear the music and taste the delicious brine, luminous around me
everywhere, green transparent light falling from upper water—
and I am loose and free as your cousin jellyfish, no longer aware of
my shell, but moving through the sea so long ago.

You are not Yorick's skull in Hamlet's hand. Now you are the
creature within me.

THE LAST BOAT-TRAIN
ON THE GREAT LAKES

The port is empty now,
the waters clear.
There are no freight sheds,
smokestacks,
trestles, gardens, ships.
There are no docks
—everything has gone back to nature.
Across the harbour the grain elevators
and a yellow generating station stand.
Up until 1990, when the government
cancelled grain subsidies,
they were still in use.

To the edge of the cracked pier
I walk past smooth, iron hawsers
which had moored the Keewatin and the Assiniboia,
ships built on the banks of the Clyde
sailed across the Atlantic,
up the St. Lawrence River
just three weeks before "The Titanic" sank.
They had to be sawed in half,
floated across Lake Ontario,
reassembled in Buffalo.

This is where my father,
a CPR conductor in the mid 50's,
rode up on the train
bringing passengers to the steamships
for weekend holiday cruises to Fort Arthur and Port William.

He sold Club Soda
to businessmen in swivel seats
who mixed it with outlawed liquor.
On weekends, he waited
for their return,
fishing from the docks,
sleeping in the caboose.

Now the ships are ghosts,
pictures in souvenir books.
My father, with his 35 mm camera,
filmed the steamship with the boat train.
When Oma visited
we stood before the waiting train
pretending to be waving crazily at relatives
embarking on a transatlantic crossing.
We waved to the crew raising the gangplank,
and I looked up at the smokestack
as the foghorn bellowed
—one of the last cruises on the Great Lakes.
Beyond the docks, I remember the sign,
"One mile to Paradise Point."

Now, I turn back and look
for the tracks,
but they are gone.
Along the cinder path I walk
and in the weeds find
a hidden imprint of tracks,
a fossil of the ties.
Beyond is the lever for the red signal.
I push it down

as if to change it back to
that other time, but
it's stuck.
Farther along I find a track fastener
shaped like home plate
and on a concrete pylon
two railway spikes.

READING THE WATER

I recollect weekend trips, my father following
red and yellow lines on maps
to obscure places with aboriginal names,
trips that began on forlorn bridges
rivers that suddenly
disappeared into tangled undergrowth,
narrowed to open fields and high grasses.
He had strategies that I could only imagine
as he followed the curves of the river,
a soldier on a subversive campaign,
recalling something no doubt mother had said
that drove him away from his family
to these hedge-lined fields
where the water was black and rushing.
He stood in the water, hip waders against
the current and waited
for the speckled, the brown, the rainbow,
moving slowly, until
he chose the right fly, the appropriate angle,
lassoing the line,

casting it out into an "s" above the current,
tugging at it
playing the waters with his fingers,
reading its bubbles as notes on some aqua score,
reading the sounds, the currents, the silences,
marks on a rippling dark page.
He waited for the change in tension.
Timing was all.
He could wait there,
wait there almost
all morning—or so it seemed,
and I followed him, continually onward,
to catch that fish.

FISHING ON THE RIVER WYE

I

At the tip of the promontory I stand, casting
with my father, into the waters of Midland Bay.
He is patient. He knows where the fish swim.
I loop the line out
into the dark hollow of the water
where it is still, and wait.

Thirty years ago, long before the marina,
we rowed over a wreck with its bow
protruding out of the water, an ancient Viking hull.
In the old green rowboat my father trolled, sculled
a pathway through the insects hovering
over the yellow blossoms on lily pads.

We waited in silence as hungry seagulls thronged
and shrieked through the sun-entangled trees.
The spire of the Martyrs' Shrine rose
where once priests
were scalped and burned by Iroquois,
their cries echoing through the morning.

He taught me the techniques of fishing, to
cast the line like a light lasso,
unspool without entangling,
wait for the precise moment,
taut with line between thumb and index finger, wait
for the tug. He taught me
to then release
the line, let the fish
swim with it through the water.
Of few words, especially
on fishing trips, he was more adept
in his language of hooks, sinkers and lures.

II

Late afternoon and we stand
on this windy ridge, the sun blurred
through clouds over Christian Island.
I see the edge of an iron rib
curling over the rocks,
the old boat like a beached whale.
I had swum out to the wreck, climbing
over gunnels, slipping
down into its depths where the lime light
shone in Technicolour,

golden green weeds waving their hair like mermaids.
I had explored its hulk, the rusted bolts
the corroded sides where a bass
turned its black eye toward me and swam away.
This was as close to a fish as I would get.

He will not tell his story
straight, any more than he would
chart a course for fishing.
I watch father concentrating
on the line, waiting
for the tug as he searches
the rising and falling
of the waves. He does not move
quickly, changes his strategy
to read the shifting wind.
He does not speak.
Beyond silence I read meaning
in his fingers, his arms, his eyes.

INTENSIVE CARE

For more than a week
you have lain in this sealed ward,
a thick tube stuck in your mouth.
Your nose, bashed like a boxer's in a late round,
has dried blood across it.
Your white hair is pushed back
like an old Jewish prophet's.

You labour to breathe.
Your eyes, drugged on morphine,
stare at the ceiling, now and then
closing so slightly.
I say, "I am here."
Your eyes try to speak.
Your lips try to open, but
only quiver.

I know there are words
beyond the tubes and catheter,
residual words rising from
within the river of your being,
the words you are trying to voice,
something of your life
that you did not say
or could not say—
and why, like a fighter,
you hold on for seven days to this life.

You are tough
—tougher than I thought.
        Your arms larger and stronger
than I remember,
your fingers, when I hold them, are tender;
softer than expected —softer than kid leather.

Your silence speaks in this room
where machines keep you alive.
I touch you as you touch me
try to keep you here with us
a little longer.

IRISH SPRING

There are certain images that remain:
the memory of walking with my uncle and father
along a chalky road somewhere in Ireland,
the sound of water falling
through rocks, running
into a stream. It is the song of a singer
whose words I do not know.
We stop, climb down
a bank, and sip from the rusty pipe.
I smell the minerals in the water.
It is the clearest, coldest water I have ever tasted.
I watch my uncle, and then my father,
drink. The thirst and the heat vanish.
We are alone in the lighted shadows
of the trees, where the wind stirs.
I listen to the stream of the earth,
the voice of the spring
becoming my own.

Climbing the Great Wall

THE DANCER, RESTING

The dancer rests
her elbow on her knee.
The music has ended.
Perhaps she replays
the motion in her mind.
This is what she does
gives herself up to motion.

The sculptor
shows her
resting,
but see the graceful
turning, how her desire is
in her limbs
contained—
see how she moves before the court
release in that moment
desire
and art
one and the same,
                    turning . . .

It is in the reaching
of her body,
the movement of her legs—
the moment in her mind, the gesture.
She has just performed

the dance of her life,
poised in this moment of rest,
                    and the remnants of the dance . . .

CHINESE EROTIC SCENE
AT THE ROYAL ONTARIO MUSEUM

After passing by the bronze horses,
vases, bowls—*lei,* suddenly
in the first or second century,
in the Eastern Han Dynasty,
a scene on the grey stone sculpted,
a man is making love to a woman
on a carpet of the forest.
A group of onlookers stands before it:
"It's a picture of a rape scene
or a prostitute, with men waiting,"
one woman cries out.
"Oh, I don't like that one!" says another.
"Let's go on to the good times."
The group is embarrassed and wants
to move on. The guide leading
the group away murmurs:
"Perhaps these are the good times."
Beside me, a professor of Chinese says:
"This work was banned in Fort Leavenworth."
It is all in grey, finely etched;
the man is about to enter the woman,
a basket and cane beside her,
her legs slide over his shoulders,
 (so long ago)
and his smaller friend behind him
slowly pushes his buttocks:
"What are friends for?" says the professor of Chinese.
And the woman's clothes dangle in the branches
in the sunlit afternoon, as the monkeys

chatter above them, peering
down, enjoying their fun,
and the peacock spreads his feathers.

It's afternoon.
The third man stands behind the tall tree
with an erection.
There is a buzz in the air.
It's late afternoon and sunny.
Perhaps this is a fertility rite or a legend.
Who knows now?
—somewhere in a warm afternoon
in the late second century AD in China.

YANG GUI FEI

In the November morning
the pagodas are outlined in frost.
The steam of the Huaqing hot springs
rises to the trees, distilling crystals
into patterns of porcelain,
cold lace over the trees
before the range of the Li Mountains.

It's morning—the first sunlight breaks
through; snow twinkles in a fire in the frost,
and the young girls from the provinces
frolic in the snow.
They are from the south
and do not know what snow is,
and take it in their fingers,
rolling it into balls,
laughing as they throw them at one another
—four or five girls having their first snow fight.
And then crackling the air
the solemn voice of the imperial concubine
freezes them into silence.
"Silly provincial girls . . .
What are you doing?
The snow is not a toy."
She raises her silky sleeve toward the sky, stopping
the flight of snowflakes.
"How can you compare the whiteness of this snow,"
 rolling up her red brocade sleeve,
"to the brilliance of this skin.
This is closer to heaven."

She drops her sleeve like a breeze
moving slowly and formally away,
the sun already melting the snow on the stones
as she strolls toward her crab apple bath
where she will bathe alone
waiting for her emperor.

THE DEATH OF YANG GUI FEI

Yang Gui Fei is the emperor's favourite.
She is from the south.
Not only is she beautiful,
she has many talents:
plays musical instruments,
writes poetry, dances.
She is very intelligent.

She controls the emperor's mind.
With her the affairs of the state are forgotten.
Her relatives are promoted to high places
and the people become very jealous.
They kill many of her family in the palace.
The generals come to the emperor and say:
You will die, if you do not kill
your favourite concubine, Yang Gui Fei.

At night the emperor crosses
through the shadows of the camp to her tent
and takes a last look at her.
He says nothing, noticing
the white plaited rope
like a necklace upon her pillow
and kisses her goodbye.

Yang Gui Fei knows the soldiers
are waiting for her, and knows
she will never see the sun again.
She watches the emperor close the netting
and walk slowly—more slowly

than she has ever seen him walk.
Lifting up the thread in her fingers
she sees the soldier's dark face outside,
the moon glimmering icily over the slopes of Mawei.

ONE OF THE FARMERS WHO DISCOVERED THE TERRA-COTTA ARMY

He sits there, shyly, behind the books
about the Terra-Cotta Army,
his face bronzed with sunlight
from his lifetime as a farmer,
his hair straight as a Chinese crew cut.
There is sharpness in his eyes
his bearing modest, yet
something in his look that says
he has done something.
Now on display
he sits crouched, looking at us
briefly, then turns away.
"There was that day in 1974," our guide, David, says,
"digging in the persimmon field south of the village.
Two other farmers and he were digging a well
and hit a jar, and in the cavity they found pieces of a 'pottery man.'
They were sent to Beijing archaeologists
and a report came back.
They had perhaps found the fabled Terra-Cotta Army."
The farmer signs the book.
I ask him, "How did you feel
discovering this army?"
A woman translates my question:
"We were very excited," he smiles.
How do you feel today about this?
"I am very proud because
I will be remembered."
He smiles and folds his hands.
"How much did he get for this discovery?"
I ask David.
"About ten yuan."

THE TERRA-COTTA WARRIORS

They are there, what is left
of Emperor Qin Shi Huang's great army,
a testament to his power.
They are defending his city
long after his death.
They are in battle formation.
The first row of warriors has no armour,
nor do they wear helmets.
They are armed with only their bravery,
their readiness to fight.
Each figure is actual size,
modelled on a warrior,
faces tough, wise, fair,
faces of professional soldiers
you might have seen in a bar
2,200 years ago.

Now you try to read their individual lives,
the particular lines in their faces,
row after row, restored in perfect formation,
their uniforms no longer coloured.
They are in columns, separated by rows of earth.
There are four horses, strong creatures
trained for battle, yet if you look farther back
you see the formation is broken
the terra-cotta soldiers not whole,
but pieces, fragments
almost as if they had died in some battle,
pierced by spears, or arrows from crossbows, fallen
to their knees or decapitated, their bodies

decaying in the dust, in the fragments
of wheels, the dust of the wooden chariots,
the leather straps.

Once the beams of a roof protected them;
now they crumble, yet even in their destruction
we imagine their lives, their dedication, their selflessness.
So many things we don't know about their lives:

at home in bed with their wives,
playing with a young son or daughter,
in the garden by the gold fish pools, perhaps
with their own little terra-cotta soldiers,
cutting the flowers in the gardens,
eating grapes with their lovers,
sitting alone in the still coolness of the temple
sipping wine with their friends, waiting
for the next battle,
concern in their eyes and fear.
If we look beyond the mask of the soldiers,
we see that it was not all war, see
ourselves in them, hear their lips speak,
"We'll live beyond this battle,
live to triumph, to drink and love again."

CLIMBING THE GREAT WALL

I

Now I am standing by these bricks of the parapet,
overlooking the valleys and the mountains.
I walk into the guardhouse
and stand here in the cool air,
look at the ancient fireplace.
I see before me boys playing cards, waiting
as the ancient guard had waited . . .

We dragged in firewood
from slopes, always on the lookout for the enemy,
watching the far fires
of comrades in the distance,
waiting for the signal,
signs of the invading army.
Here, we would wait under the cold stars,
so distant from wives,
born to this soldier's life
in service of the dragon
better than bearing stones
up mountains with donkeys,
sometimes the men dying in the heat.
We think of our comrades.
We tell stories of old battles,
of friends no longer here,
of father gone to the place of ancestors.
We play games with the emperor's dice;
it keeps us warm at night.

I think of my wife,
her body under silk,
our desire to be together.
Yet we are so solitary in the night,
only the voices from the guardhouses,
voices of our comrades fallen in battle,
and those who died building these walls.

These walls are our safety—
They bind the country.
They are our way of life.
They follow the mountains.
They are the mountains.
They are the skeleton.
They are the dragons.

Sometimes, late at night under the call of eagles,
under the frosty moon, I listen
and write my thoughts down.
We are forgotten at the outpost.
We are here, guarding the country.
                    Remember our lives.
We could give you our names
but you would not remember them.

II

I reach the base guardhouse
and I stop, my heart racing beneath my rib cage.
I must go on.
"It's only 423 steps," one student says.
"Lean forward or you will fall back."
"You just have to keep going."

It's as steep as a Mayan temple.
I begin the climb, step by step.
It is harder, slower than I thought,
like moving in another element.
I look up and begin to count to pass the time,
as I did as a kid on my old *Globe and Mail* route,
or when I'm shovelling the snow from my driveway.
No, I must experience this
heat, pain, uncertainty
—they are part of the wall.

Upward I move toward the summit.
The last twenty steps I climb slowly,
not leaning back, and secure my steps.
Here I am at the summit of Mitianyu
see the wall weave like a dragon's tail among the mountains.
And here I stand, before the still gate,
the broken remnants of the wall.

Then I look up and see
an eagle veer out of the clouds,
its sleek white form. How high it is.
I watch it curve and rise in a spiral
as it winds up the mountain of air.
Then another eagle joins it in its circle,
and they fly, tracing circles,
skaters making figure eights,
weaving in their mutual symmetry,
flying high above the Great Wall over China.

BIOGRAPHY

Laurence Hutchman has published seven books of poetry, including his most recent *Selected Poems*. In 2007 he received the Alden Nowlan Award for Excellence in English-language Literary Arts. He teaches English Literature at the Université de Moncton in Edmundston where he lives with his wife, Mary.

AWARDS

—Alden Nowlan Award for Excellence in English-language Literary Arts, 2007
—First prize, poetry category, Writers' Federation of New Brunswick, Literary Competition, 2006
—Third prize, poetry category, Writers' Federation of New Brunswick, Literary Competition, 1997
—Honourable mention for the Alfred Bailey Prize in 1995

PUBLICATIONS

Selected Poems (2007)
Coastlines: The Poetry of Atlantic Canada (2002) (co-editor)
Beyond Borders (2000)
Emery (1998)
Foreign National (1993)
Blue Riders (1985),
Explorations (1975)
The Twilight Kingdom (1973)